A book for
thought ~
A nook for
rest ~:

Suzanne Leupold Doyle

December '83

To Suzanne Doyle
Enjoy these gifts
from the kitchen all
year 'round!

Emily Cumpackn

SEASONAL GIFTS
from the
KITCHEN

Emily Crumpacker

Illustrated by
Vivienne Flesher

William Morrow and Company, Inc.
New York 1983

For W. Boyd Smith

*

Seasonal Gifts
from the Kitchen

by Emily Crumpacker

Illustrations by Vivienne Flesher

*

*

We gratefully acknowledge permission to reprint "Preserved Lemons" (page 31) from COUSCOUS AND OTHER GOOD FOOD by Paula Wolfert, copyright © 1973 by Paula Wolfert, Reprinted by permission of Harper & Row, Publishers, Inc. and "Pâte de Framboises" in FRENCH REGIONAL COOKING by Anne Willan, copyright © 1981 by Marshall Editions Limited, text copyright © 1981 by Anne Willan & l'Ecole de Cuisine La Varenne by permission of William Morrow & Company.

Library of Congress Catalog Card Number: 83-61796

ISBN: 0-688-02569-2

Copyright © 1983 Smallwood & Stewart

Produced by Smallwood & Stewart,
6 Alconbury Rd., London E.5.

Design by Larry Kazal

Printed and bound in Italy
by A. Mondadori, Verona

First Edition
1 2 3 4 5 6 7 8 9 10

Contents

THE WRITING OF THIS BOOK

began with my awareness of the abundance of gifts that can be made in the kitchen. Although it seems that today almost any delicacy can be found on the shelves of supermarkets and gourmet stores, the most interesting and memorable foods are still those made at home. Despite the claim on the label, there is nothing like 'homemade,' and there is no doubt that you can achieve an individuality, variety, and freshness in your kitchen that no store-bought gift can offer. For me, the pure pleasure to be had preparing these foods is more than equalled by the appreciation of friends and relatives on receiving something made specially for them.

But a cookbook really begins with a love of food and cooking: the appreciation I learned from my grandmother's creative yet realistic approach to cooking; my university training; the love and respect for food taught by Chambrette, Claude, Jorant, and all at La Varenne; and Simca Beck's delightful, adventurous attitude to cooking. They have all, in their way, contributed to this book.

In selecting recipes I have been careful to maintain a balance between the interesting and unusual and the straightforward to prepare. Few require numerous exotic ingredients or lengthy procedures; those that do are well worth the effort! As the title suggests, the recipes are organized with an eye to using fruits

and vegetables at their best, when they are in season. Although
it seems now that most produce is available all year round, there is no
question that quality and price are better during its 'season.' At
the same time, the seasonal divisions are not rigid, and there are many
recipes that can be made throughout the year.

Most of the recipes can, of course,
be varied. Sometimes I have included a few suggestions, but you may
find that you want to use a little less sugar or a pinch more of the
spices or another garlic clove, for example, to meet your own taste.
Cooking is something of an inexact science: your batch of plums may be
very large or juicy, your herbs fresher and more flavorful, your
raspberries sweeter, so the yields, seasonings, and cooking times are
only close approximations. Occasionally you may find you have
sterilized too many jars, or that a jam needs a little longer cooking, but
generally these should be reliable guidelines. Except in the few cases
where it is indicated in the recipe butter is always sweet, at room
temperature, eggs are medium-sized, at room temperature; and flour
is all-purpose.

Hopefully this selection of my
favorite recipes will give you as much enjoyment as I have received
from them over the years and will inspire you to invent some of your
own gifts from the kitchen.

Spring

ALMOND
CARROT
JAM

runchy and tart, almond carrot jam is a perfect foil for robust game dishes. Adjust the amount of sugar to taste; and try using other herbs (tarragon or basil), or spices (nutmeg or cumin), adding a little at a time and checking for flavor.

*1 lb carrots * ³/₄ cup sugar*

*juice of 2 lemons * zest of 1 lemon*

¹/₃ cup blanched almonds, quartered

2 tbs brandy

METHOD: Peel and trim the carrots. Cut into ¹/₂-inch slices, place in a saucepan, and just cover with cold water. Simmer slowly until the carrots are tender. Drain and put through a fine sieve or food mill.

In a saucepan, combine the carrot puree, sugar, lemon juice and zest, and almonds. Bring the mixture to a boil, reduce heat, and simmer for 15 minutes. Stir in the brandy (to prevent spoilage) and turn into jars. Seal tightly and store in a cool, dry place. *Yield: 2–3 cups*

RHUBARB-
ORANGE
COMPOTE

*d*elicious with a few toasted nuts sprinkled on top for breakfast, or as the base for a fruit tart, or as a cake filling, this recipe is simplicity itself. Store in a tightly sealed jar in the refrigerator for a week; frozen, it will keep for 6 months.

3 cups rhubarb,
trimmed and cut into 1-inch pieces

⅓ cup water ∗ 3–5 tbs sugar

2 tbs Grand Marnier or orange juice

2–3 drops red food coloring (optional)

METHOD: Heat the rhubarb and water in a heavy-based saucepan over medium heat stirring frequently, for 10 minutes, until most of the rhubarb has lost its shape. (It is best to leave the mixture a little chunky.) Remove from heat and stir in the sugar a tablespoon at a time, until the desired sweetness has been reached. Add the Grand Marnier or orange juice and stir in the food coloring a drop at a time. Pile into prepared jars and cover tightly. *Yield: 1½–2 cups*

SWEET
EASTER
BREAD

prinkled with toasted, sliced almonds, this rich fruit bread is traditional at our family Easter table. Wrapped in plastic or foil, the bread freezes very well.

½ cup raisins

¼ cup brandy * *¼ cup hot water*

1 pkg dry yeast * *¾ cup warm water (110°F)*

⅓ cup sugar * *½ cup butter* * *4 eggs*

1 tsp vanilla * *½ tsp salt*

zest of 2 oranges

4½ cups flour

For the glaze: 1 egg beaten with 1 tbs water

For the icing: ¼ cup orange juice
¼ cup sugar

METHOD: Cover the raisins with the brandy and ¼ cup hot water; set aside. In a small bowl, mix the yeast, ¾ cup warm water, and a tablespoon sugar together. Set aside until bubbles appear on the surface and mixture swells. Beat the butter and remaining sugar together. Add the eggs one by one, beating well

after each addition. Mix in the vanilla, salt, and orange zest, then the yeast mixture. Add 2 cups of flour and beat well with a wooden spoon. Work in 2 more cups of flour. Turn the dough out onto a floured board (using the remaining ½ cup flour) and knead for 10 minutes, until smooth and elastic, adding flour if necessary to prevent sticking. Shape into a smooth ball and place in a large, buttered bowl, turning to coat completely with butter. Cover and set in a warm place for 1½ hours, until doubled in size.

Punch dough down and turn onto a lightly floured board. Drain the raisins, add to the dough, and knead for 4-5 minutes. Shape into a smooth ball and place on a greased, sideless baking sheet. Roll out into a 10-inch round, cover, and let double in size again. Make 2 cuts across the top of the loaf, about ⅛ inch deep. Brush the top with egg glaze.

Bake in a 350°F oven for 30 minutes, or until the loaf has browned nicely. While the bread is baking, make the icing. Combine the sugar and orange juice in a saucepan. Simmer gently for 5-10 minutes, until a light syrup forms. Spoon the syrup over the bread as soon as it is removed from the oven. Cool on a wire rack. *Yield: One large loaf or two medium loaves*

SPRING

——

13

——

HERBED VODKA

Herbed liquors are always welcome and distinctive gifts. Half the fun is in experimenting: I have used a tablespoon of green peppercorns, 6 anise seeds, and even a whole garlic clove—and flavored gin and brandy as well. The flavors will mature with keeping, so try to make a week, or preferably several weeks, in advance. Add the sugar syrup only if you want a sweet, liqueur-style beverage.

1 tbs rosemary leaves

1 piece lemon peel * *4 coriander seeds, crushed*

1 bottle vodka (one fifth)

One week later (optional): 1 cup sugar * *½ cup water*

METHOD: Wash the rosemary leaves and bruise gently to release their aroma. Pare the lemon skin using a peeler and remove a piece about 6 inches long with as little of the white membrane as possible. Add the crushed coriander, rosemary leaves, and lemon peel to the vodka. Shake well and let steep for at least a week. Strain through cheesecloth and re-bottle before use. To sweeten, heat the sugar and water and boil gently for several minutes. Allow to cool before adding to the strained liquor.

MEDITERRANEAN OLIVES

*T*here are countless ways of flavoring olives, as anyone who has visited a Mediterranean food market knows. Try using dark, strongly-flavored Greek olives, or stuffing with anchovies or orange peel, or changing the flavoring by adding half a cinnamon stick, or fresh rosemary leaves, or coriander seeds.

¼ cup green olives, pitted

½ cup blanched almonds

2 small, fresh, red chili peppers or 1 tbs dried chili pepper flakes

4 cloves garlic, peeled and sliced

olive oil

METHOD: Stuff each olive with an almond and layer in a jar with chili peppers and garlic slices. Add olive oil to cover and seal the jar. Store in the refrigerator for 2 weeks before using.

SPRING

15

SALMON
TARRAGON
BUTTER

pread thinly on rounds of toasted bread, topped with a little chopped parsley or caviar, salmon butter makes marvelous canapés. In a decorated or earthenware crock it becomes a very attractive present.

1 7-oz can salmon

*5 oz good-quality smoked salmon or lox,
cut into 1-inch pieces*

¾ lb butter

*2 tbs fresh tarragon leaves,
or 2 tsp dried tarragon*

*¼ cup vodka * salt and pepper to taste*

clarified butter

METHOD: Place the salmon and smoked salmon in a food processor and blend well. Add the remaining ingredients, and salt and pepper to taste, process again, and pile into crocks. (If using a blender, add the salmon a little at a time. In a separate bowl, combine remaining ingredients with a hand mixer or whisk, then beat in the fish.) Seal with clarified butter. Store in the refrigerator for up to 2 weeks; frozen, it will keep for at least 1 month. *Yield: 2 cups*

MRS. PAMPLIN'S
ARTICHOKE
RELISH

Jerusalem artichokes are growing in popularity after several decades of neglect. They are quite easy to find and are often packaged as 'sun-chokes' in produce markets. This recipe was given to me by Mrs. Robert Pamplin, a marvelous cook and gracious hostess. Together with her husband, she tends a grand garden even producing the artichokes used in this relish. Its chunky texture and tangy flavor accompany roast game dishes or a picnic menu perfectly.

2 cups Jerusalem artichokes

*2 medium onions, sliced * ¼ head cabbage, sliced*

1 cup cauliflower, broken into flowerettes

½ bell pepper, coarsely chopped

*¼ cup salt * 1 quart water*

For the dressing:

*1 tbs dry mustard * ¾ tsp turmeric*

*⅔ cup flour * 1 cup sugar*

1⅓ cups white wine vinegar

*¾ cup water * 1 tsp celery seed*

1 tsp white mustard seed

salt and pepper to taste

SPRING

18

METHOD: Scrub the artichokes
and cut into small cubes (about ¼–½ inch).
Prepare all the other vegetables. Place the cabbage,
cauliflower, and peppers in a large stainless
steel pot. Dissolve the salt in the water to make a
brine, pour over the vegetables, and let stand
for 24 hours. Soak the artichokes and onions
separately in plain water for 24 hours. The next day,
drain off the brine into a large pan and bring
to a boil. Add all the vegetables except the
artichokes and return to a boil. Drain completely
and discard the brine. For the dressing, sift the
mustard, turmeric, flour, and sugar together in
a large saucepan. Add the vinegar and water
and cook, stirring constantly, for about 5 minutes
after it thickens. Add the celery seed, mustard
seed, and black pepper. Return to a boil, being
very careful not to scorch; add the drained
vegetables (without the artichokes), and bring the
sauce to a boil, again stirring constantly, and add
salt to taste. Remove from the heat and stir in
the artichokes. Put in sterilized jars and seal.
Yield: 4–5 cups

ROSE PETAL JAM

**L**iving in the City of Roses, Portland cooks often ask me for this recipe. This sweet-scented jam has a delicate flavor: I serve it spread thinly on morning toast or between the layers of a light cake.

20 sweet-scented roses, red and pink

6 cups sugar cubes * 4 cups water

1 cup boiling water * ½ tsp citric acid

METHOD: Gather the roses when fully open and fresh. Heat the sugar cubes with the 4 cups water until dissolved, then boil for half an hour over medium heat. Separate the petals, remove the white base of each petal, and tear in half. Place the petals in a large bowl and add 1 cup of boiling water. Stir gently, making sure all the petals are thoroughly moistened, then pour the petals and the soaking water into the boiling syrup, stirring constantly. Boil for another 30 minutes, stirring frequently with a wooden spoon, pressing the petals down into the syrup (some tend to float to the top). When the petals are tender and syrup clear, add the citric acid and boil for 10 minutes or until the mixture becomes syrupy. Pour into prepared jars and seal. *Yield: 6 cups*

RICH
CHOCOLATE
CAKE

*R*ich doesn't come close to describing this incredibly dense, delicious cake; although it is small, it will serve 8–10 people! Make it at least 3 days and up to 2 weeks before serving (it can be frozen). I often give it wrapped in a box (still in the foil) with a bottle of the cream, together with directions for serving, all tied with a big bow.

8 oz semi-sweet chocolate

*⅓ cup strong black coffee * 1 tsp vanilla*

*1 cup butter * 1 cup sugar*

4 eggs, beaten

For the cream:

*1½ cups heavy cream * 2 tbs sugar*

2 tbs brandy

METHOD: Line a 5-cup soufflé or charlotte mold with a double thickness of foil. In a large double boiler heat the chocolate and the coffee and stir until melted. Add the vanilla, butter, and sugar a little at a time, stirring after each addition, until melted. Take from the heat and beat the eggs into the chocolate gradually (an electric mixer is ideal for this).

Do not allow the eggs to stick to the sides of
the pan. Pour the mixture into the prepared mold
and bake in the middle of a 350°F oven for
about 1 hour or until a thick crust has formed
on top. The mixture will rise slightly but will
fall as it cools. Let the cake cool; cover and keep
in the refrigerator.

   Not more than 3 hours before serving, turn
the cake onto a platter and peel off the foil (it
will look very messy at this point). Beat the cream,
sugar, and brandy together until stiff, fill a
pastry bag fitted with a medium star tip and cover
the cake with rosettes. Chill until serving.

PIQUANT APRICOT CHUTNEY

*W*arm amber in color, this apricot chutney has a zesty sweet-and-sour flavor. Red chilis add the spark and chopped dates make the texture more intriguing. Be sure to use only dried apricots, not fresh, and you may want to adjust the sugar to taste.

2 cups dried apricots, chopped

1 cup dates,
pitted and coarsely chopped

1 cup brown sugar, firmly packed

1 cup sugar

1 cup cider vinegar

1 small onion, chopped

1 tablespoon fresh ginger, minced

2 small dried red chilis,
seeds removed, crushed

juice from 1 lime

1 clove garlic,
finely minced

1¼ cups water

METHOD: In a bowl, pour just enough boiling water over apricots and dates to cover and let 'plump' for at least 2 hours or overnight.

In a 4-quart stainless-steel pot, combine sugars, vinegar, onion, ginger, chilis, lime juice, garlic, and water. Bring to a boil, then reduce heat and simmer, uncovered, until mixture thickens, about 20 minutes.

Drain apricots and dates and stir into mixture. Continue cooking at a simmer for 15 to 20 minutes until fruit softens. Pour into prepared jars and store. *Yield: 5 cups*

MOROCCAN
PRESERVED
LEMONS

Almost any cook would welcome a gift of preserved lemons. They are frequently used in North African cooking, adding a salty tartness to chicken, lamb, and vegetable dishes. I was once given 20 pounds of lemons and turned to Paula Wolfert's excellent recipe below, from *Couscous and Other Good Food from Morocco*, to preserve half the gift. Make sure that you cover the lemons completely with salted lemon juice before sealing the jar. The pickling juice can be reused, and it is convenient to keep a jar in the kitchen and replenish it with odd pieces of lemon.

5 lemons

⅓ cup salt, more if desired

Optional Safi mixture:

1 cinnamon stick ✳ 3 cloves

5–6 coriander seeds

3–4 black peppercorns ✳ 1 bay leaf

freshly squeezed lemon juice, if necessary

METHOD: If you wish to soften the peel, soak the lemons in lukewarm water

for 3 days, changing the water daily. Quarter
the lemons from the top to within ½ inch of the
bottom, sprinkle salt on the exposed flesh, then
reshape the fruit.

Place 1 tbs salt on the bottom of a sterilized
1-pint mason jar. Pack in the lemons and push
them down, adding more salt, and the optional
spices, between the layers. Press the lemons down
to release their juices and to make room for the
remaining lemons. (If the juice released from the
squashed fruit does not cover them, add freshly
squeezed lemon juice—not chemically produced
lemon juice and *not* water.) Leave some air
space before sealing the jar.

Turn the jar upside down to distribute the salt
and the juice, and let the lemons ripen in a warm
place for 30 days.

To use, rinse the lemons as needed under
running water, removing and discarding the pulp,
if desired; there is no need to refrigerate after
opening. Preserved lemons will keep up to a year,
and the pickling juice can be used two or three
times over the course of a year. *Yield: 2 cups*

Summer

RASPBERRY
VINEGAR

aspberries,
blackberries, gooseberries, even strawberries all
add an irresistible flavor to vinegars that will
bring to life a vinaigrette or a light fish sauce.
Follow the same method below for herbed
vinegars, too, using a couple of sprigs of rosemary,
basil, or tarragon; or a tablespoon of green
peppercorns, 4–5 peeled cloves or garlic, 3–4 dried
chili peppers, or a combination of these. Strain
and add fresh herbs or fruit to the vinegar as a
decoration before giving.

1 cup fresh berries, washed and picked over

4 cups good quality white wine vinegar

⅓ cup sugar

METHOD: Put the berries
in a 5-cup jar or bottle. Heat the vinegar and sugar
together until the sugar dissolves. Pour into
the jar and mash the berries to release their flavor.
Seal tightly and set aside in a dark, cool place
for at least 2 weeks before using. Strain before
use. *Yield: 5 cups*

PLUM
TOMATO
RELISH

uring the peak of
the season I always make a batch of this relish
to use with meat dishes or barbecues.

*6 lbs ripe plum tomatoes * 1 large onion, chopped*

*2 tsp mustard seed * 2 tsp black peppercorns*

*2 tsp dried basil leaves * 1 tsp whole allspice*

*1 small dried hot chili pepper * 1 bay leaf*

*½ stick cinnamon * ¾ cup brown sugar*

*1½ tsp salt * 1½ tsp paprika * ½ cup vinegar*

METHOD: Coarsely chop 5
lbs of the tomatoes and blend, a small amount
at a time, with the onion until very smooth.
Press through a strainer into a 4-quart pot and
discard the pulp. You should have 2–2½ quarts
of puree. Bring to a boil and simmer uncovered
over medium heat, stirring occasionally, until it is
reduced by half. Tie the mustard seed, peppercorns,
basil, allspice, chili, bay leaf, and cinnamon in
cheesecloth and add to the puree. Cook over
medium heat, adding the sugar, salt, and paprika,
stirring often until it is reduced by half again.
Add the vinegar, cook another 10 minutes, and
discard the spice bag. Peel and de-seed the
remaining pound of tomatoes, chop coarsely, and
stir into the relish. Cook 5 minutes. Cool
and pour into containers. *Yield: 4–5 cups*

BLACK CHERRIES IN COGNAC

weet, dark cherries are usually available in the markets from May through August. Preserving them in cognac or brandy for the rest of the year is quite easy, and a very similar method can be followed to preserve most fresh fruits (and many dried fruits, too) all year round. Dried fruits—prunes, peaches, apricots—should be re-hydrated by soaking them in water overnight before adding to the boiling sugar syrup.

Fruit preserved this way can be served with a dessert or, of course, on its own. Cherries in cognac go well with pork, duck, and even poached fish. Kept tightly sealed and stored in a cool, dark place, preserved fruits will keep for up to 8 months.

5 cups sugar

2 cups water

1 vanilla bean

*3 lbs cherries, washed and stemmed;
and pitted, if preferred*

2 cups cognac

METHOD: Boil the sugar and
water together with the vanilla bean to form a
clear syrup (about 8 minutes). Remove the bean,
and pour over the cherries. Let stand overnight.
The next day, drain the syrup and slowly
bring to a boil. Add the fruit and boil gently
for 8 minutes. Lift the cherries out with a slotted
spoon and pack into sterilized jars. Boil the
syrup down until quite thick; while it is boiling
add the cognac. Immediately pour over the
cherries. Cover and seal. *Yield: 3 pints*

JULY 4th
GINGER
CAKE

he texture is similar to that of a pound cake, but the flavor is a refreshing surprise. When you give this cake, suggest serving it with fresh summer fruits and heavy cream whipped with a little sugar and brandy. Well-wrapped, ginger cake keeps one week but can be successfully frozen.

¾ cup butter

*¾ cup sugar * 3 eggs * 1¼ cup flour*

*2 tbs baking powder * 1 tsp vanilla*

¼ cup preserved ginger, finely chopped, dredged in flour

METHOD: Cream the butter and sugar together and beat in the eggs one at a time, mixing well after each addition. Sift the flour and baking powder together and stir into the sugar mixture one third at a time. Add the vanilla and ginger. Pour the batter into a buttered, floured, 8-inch cake pan and bake in a 325°F oven for 45 minutes, or until the middle springs back when touched. Remove from the oven; allow to cool for several minutes, then remove from pan and cool on a rack.

SWEET
PICKLED
PEACHES

I make this classic
recipe when the fruit is at its most plentiful,
choosing only the smallest and firmest peaches.
Add 2 or 3 whole allspice, or even a teaspoon of
green peppercorns if you want to vary the recipe.
Serve halved with cold meats, or sliced and mixed
with sour cream in a chicken salad.

4 lbs peaches

3 whole cloves for each peach ∗ 2 cups cider vinegar

3 cups sugar ∗ 1 tbs whole cloves

METHOD: Skin the peaches by
dipping them briefly in boiling water and sliding
the skins off with a knife. Stick 3 whole cloves
in each peach. Mix the cider vinegar with the
sugar in a large pot, add the tablespoon of cloves,
and bring to a boil. Place the peaches in the
boiling mixture and boil rapidly for 10 minutes or
until the peaches are tender when pierced. Remove
the peaches with a slotted spoon and place
in hot sterile jars. Pour the cooked vinegar over
the peaches and seal.
   If your pot is not large enough to contain
all the peaches at one time, boil a few at a time and
continue to boil in the vinegar mixture until
all are done. *Yield: 4 pints*

RASPBERRY PASTILLES

in France this recipe is made with black currants, and I have adapted Anne Willan's recipe for *pâte de cassis*, from her excellent *French Regional Cooking*, to use raspberries. These delectable little jellies can be cut into fancy shapes and served with a glass of kir (white wine and a tablespoon of *cassis*), or lemonade on a summer's afternoon. Store in an airtight container in a cool place.

*2 lbs raspberries (approximately 3 pints),
washed and picked over*

*2²/₃ cups sugar * sugar for rolling*

METHOD: Lightly oil an 8-inch cake pan. Put the raspberries in a saucepan, cover, and simmer until the fruit can be easily mashed to a pulp. Remove from the heat and push through a sieve. Return to the pan, stir in the sugar, and heat gently until dissolved. Boil for 20-25 minutes, stirring constantly with a wooden spoon and skimming occasionally, until the mixture comes away from the sides of the pan and reaches 230°F on a sugar thermometer. Pour into the oiled pan. Leave in a cool place for several days. Cut into about 1-inch cubes (or shapes) and roll in sugar. *Yield: about 1½ lbs*

PESTO

esto is commonly
served over pasta, but it can also be used over
fish, meat, salads, or in soup. To remove some of
its harshness, I blanch fresh basil for about
10 seconds in boiling water and rinse under cold
water before use. A variation is to substitute
half the basil with parsley and use blanched
almonds instead of pine nuts. To freeze, combine
the basil and olive oil only and add the other
ingredients before use. Refrigerated, pesto will
keep for several days.

2 cups fresh basil leaves,
washed and stems removed

¾ cup olive oil

½ cup parmesan cheese, finely grated

¼ cup pine nuts

3 cloves garlic, peeled and mashed

*⅓ cup warm water * salt and pepper*

METHOD: Put the leaves in
a blender and add olive oil and all the other
ingredients. Blend until smooth. Season to taste.
Store in a tightly sealed container. *Yield: 1 cup*
(enough for 1 lb fettucine)

SPICY PEANUT SAUCE

Many Oriental and Middle Eastern dishes include peanut sauces, and friends love to receive this one as a gift because it is so versatile. I usually serve it warm, surrounded by an arrangement of raw vegetables. Adjust the consistency, if you wish, by increasing or decreasing the water. Tightly sealed, it will keep indefinitely in the refrigerator.

1 cup fresh smooth peanut butter

½ cup hot water

2 cloves garlic, finely minced and mashed

*2 tbs soy sauce * 1 tsp ground cumin*

¼ tsp cayenne powder

½ tsp curry powder

1 tsp fresh lemon juice

METHOD: In the blender, whisk all the ingredients together to form a smooth paste. Cover and set aside for several hours to allow the flavors to mix well. Turn into jars and seal; store in the refrigerator. *Yield: 1½–2 cups*

BASTILLE
DAY
GALETTE

This is a variation of the fruit tart I made for the first time to celebrate Bastille Day (July 14) with French friends in Portland. The crisp, nutty flavor goes well with an espresso or a glass of iced mint tea.

Choose any flavor of good quality sweet preserves for the topping, and if you plan to make this a few days in advance, keep the galette in a tightly sealed tin and brush with the warmed preserves just before serving.

2 cups toasted, chopped hazelnuts
(¹/₂ cup for topping)

*1 cup flour * ¹/₂ cup sugar*

¹/₂ cup butter

For the topping: ¹/₂ cup sweet preserves

METHOD: Toast the hazelnuts in a 400°F oven on a baking sheet for 5–7 minutes, shaking the sheet frequently so that they do not burn. Remove from the oven and rub a few at a time in a clean dish towel to remove as much of the husks as possible. Put the toasted nuts ¹/₂ cup at a time into a blender and grind until fine. Return 1¹/₂ cups of the nuts to the blender with ¹/₂ cup of flour; blend to mix. Add the

remaining flour and mix for a few seconds. Mix
the sugar and butter together in a large bowl
until pasty. Continue to mix, adding the flour and
nut mixture a little at a time. When the mixture
is smooth, wrap in wax paper and refrigerate
for 1 hour.

Divide the dough into 3 parts and pat into
7–inch rounds on 2 baking sheets (using a flan
ring will help shape the dough). Bake in a 375°F
oven for 10–12 minutes, until golden brown at the
edges. While the rounds are still warm, cut
into 8 wedges.

Before serving, warm the preserves in a pan
and brush each slice with a thin coating. Sandwich
the slices, preserve sides together, and brush
the top with more of the preserves. Finally,
sprinkle with the remaining ½ cup toasted,
chopped hazelnuts. *Yield: 12 servings*

BLUEBERRY PECAN CORN MUFFINS

orn muffins have been family favorites for three generations: to my grandmother's original recipe, my mother added pecans, and I've put in the blueberries.

1 1/2 cups cornmeal

*1/2 cup flour * 1 tbs sugar*

*1/2 tsp salt * 3 tbs baking powder*

*3 eggs * 1 1/4 cup milk*

1/3 cup melted butter

3/4 cup coarsely chopped pecans

1/2 cup fresh blueberries

METHOD: Butter muffin tins and set aside. Sift the cornmeal, flour, sugar, salt, and baking powder together in a large bowl. Beat the eggs with the milk and combine with the dry ingredients, using a wooden spoon. Add the melted butter, chopped pecans, and blueberries. Mix well and fill muffin tins. Bake 12–15 minutes in a 400°F oven, and turn onto a rack to cool. Store the muffins in the freezer and warm by placing them in a brown paper bag in a 250°F oven for 20 minutes. *Yield: 1 dozen muffins*

SUMMER MELBA SAUCE

Fresh raspberries in January? . . . very nearly with Melba sauce prepared during the summer when the berries are at their peak. It is sensational over poached peaches, baked custards, or as a bed for grapefruit sherbet.

2 pints fresh raspberries,
washed and stemmed

½ cup superfine sugar

1 tbs lemon juice

2 tbs kirsch

METHOD: Mash the berries in a bowl and put them through a food mill or a fine sieve to remove all the seeds. Stir in the sugar, lemon juice, and kirsch. Pour into a jar, tightly cover, and store in the refrigerator; to keep for more than a couple of days, freeze.
Yield: 2 cups

Autumn

FIG
ALMOND
RELISH

During autumn, the tree outside our kitchen window is laden with figs, and I always make this relish. The unusual combination of the almond texture with the sweet fig flavor will bring a cold meat dish or a mild curry to life.

2½ lbs fresh figs,
stems discarded and cut into ¼-inch slices

*2 cups sugar * ⅓ cup orange juice * zest from one orange*

1 cinnamon stick, broken into small pieces

*2 whole cloves * 2 whole allspice*

⅓ cup cider vinegar

½ cup almonds, coarsely chopped and toasted

METHOD: In a 4-quart
stainless-steel pot, combine the figs, sugar, orange juice, and zest. Allow to stand at room temperature for 2–3 hours. Place the spices in cheesecloth and tie tightly. Bring the fruit mixture to a boil. Reduce heat, add spice bag and vinegar. Simmer gently, stirring carefully, for 30 minutes. Add almonds and remove from heat. Remove spices and cool; pour into prepared jars and seal. *Yield: 2½ cups*

CHESTNUT
JAM
POMAINE

hether folded into whipped heavy cream and piled into a meringue shell or added to a stuffing for the Thanksgiving turkey, chestnut jam is delicious. If you wish to use fresh chestnuts, follow the directions for preparing them in "Chocolate Chestnut Truffles," page 64. Chestnut jam keeps for 2-3 months in a tightly sealed jar, but it's so tasty that it never seems to be around more than a week or two.

2 lbs canned chestnuts,
or 2½ lbs fresh

1 lb sugar cubes

vanilla bean

METHOD: Drain the chestnuts and put them through a food mill fitted with a medium ricing disc. In a heavy-based saucepan, dissolve the sugar with ½ cup water over medium heat. Wash down the sides of the pan with a brush dipped in cold water. Reduce heat, add the vanilla bean, cover, and cook the syrup for 15 minutes. Stir 1½ cups water into the chestnuts. Blend well, then add to the syrup. Simmer for another 20 minutes, stirring constantly. Remove the vanilla bean and put the jam into warmed jars. Seal tightly. *Yield: 3–4 cups*

WILD BLACKBERRY BRANDY

fresh fruit liquors bear no comparison to the fruit-flavored brandies and liqueurs available in the stores. Start with fresh fruit and a good quality liquor—brandy, vodka, gin—and it is almost impossible not to end up with something good! They keep well and continue to mature for several months, until they are strained, so make well in advance. The variations are endless; with soft fruits like raspberries, blackberries, black currants, or blueberries, follow the method below; strawberries, cranberries, cherries, and other fruits with tougher skins should be pricked before marinating in the liquor. Adjust sugar to taste. Try combinations like orange-cranberry, raspberry-peach, or anise-blueberry.

4 cups blackberries,
washed and picked over

2 cups brandy

One week later:

*1½ cups water * 1 cup sugar*

1 cup brandy

METHOD: Crush the
blackberries in a bowl and pour into a jar. Add
the 2 cups of brandy and shake well to mix.
Seal tightly and store in a cool, dry place for one
week. Heat the sugar and water together until the
sugar is dissolved. Set aside to cool. Strain the
berry brandy 2 or 3 times through a double layer
of cheesecloth, making sure to squeeze all the
liquid out of the pulp. Stir the cup of brandy
and the sugar syrup into the strained berry-
brandy. Pour into prepared bottles. *Yield:
approximately 4 cups*

COINTREAU
CHOCOLATE
SAUCE

 search for the perfect chocolate sauce . . . many ideas and concoctions later . . . this simple mixture of four ingredients fills the bill. Versatile and quite special, it can be served over fresh strawberries, poached pears, or a vanilla soufflé. Grand Marnier, Cognac, Amaretto, or any liqueur can be substituted for Cointreau, but if no liqueur is desired, increase cream by ⅓ cup instead.

1 cup heavy cream

10 oz semi-sweet chocolate, chopped

3 tbs butter

⅓ cup Cointreau

METHOD: In a heavy-based saucepan, bring the cream to a simmer. Remove from heat, add the chocolate and butter, and whisk until the mixture is smooth. Stir in the Cointreau. Pour into warmed jars and store in the refrigerator; the sauce will keep for several months. To serve, reheat in a double boiler. *Yield: 2 cups*

CARAMELIZED
ALMOND
CLUSTERS

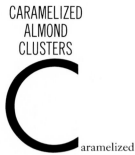

Caramelized
almonds make special gifts at any time of year.
I often hand them around on a plate with a variety
of chocolates after dinner, with coffee. Quickly and
easily prepared, the finished candies are beautiful,
but it is important that they be kept in an airtight
container to prevent them from becoming sticky.

¾ cup almonds, unblanched

½ cup sugar

METHOD: Put the sugar
and nuts into a heavy-based saucepan over
medium heat and stir until the sugar starts to melt.
Continue to cook, stirring frequently with a
wooden spoon, until the sugar is a dark caramel
color. Dip the bottom of the pan quickly
into cold water to stop the cooking; remove
immediately. Drop small spoonfuls of the nut
mixture (about 3–4 nuts in each) onto an oiled
baking sheet. Allow to cool, then transfer
immediately to an airtight container. Layer with
wax paper and keep tightly sealed. *Yield:
1–1½ dozen candies*

APPLE
CHILI
CHUTNEY

erved cold
or slightly heated, this mild chutney is a perfect
accompaniment to cold meats, game, or just bread
and cheese. You should let it mellow for at
least 2 weeks before using as the flavor will improve
with keeping. Increase the garlic or ginger
if you would like it spicier.

*2½ lbs cooking apples,
peeled and finely chopped*

*1⅓ cups brown sugar * 2 cups malt or cider vinegar*

*1 small onion, finely chopped * 2 cloves garlic, minced*

*1 small piece of ginger (about 1½ inches long)
peeled and finely grated*

*½ cup currants * ½ tsp mustard seed*

4 green chilis, finely chopped and de-seeded

METHOD: In a 4-quart
stainless-steel pot bring apples, brown sugar, and
vinegar to simmer and cook over medium
heat until the apples are soft, about 15 minutes.
Add onion, garlic, ginger, currants, mustard seed,
and chilis. Simmer uncovered until thick and
pulpy, about 20 minutes. Cool and bottle.
Yield: about 4 cups

SHERRY-CRANBERRY JELLY

his is just
a little different from the traditional relish for
Thanksgiving. Served cold, perhaps garnished
with fresh mint or a little freshly grated nutmeg,
it is a perfect addition to pork or game dishes
as well as turkey. Tightly sealed, this tart jelly
will keep in the refrigerator for several months.

2 cups dry white wine

1 quart cranberries, washed and picked over

*2 cups sugar * pinch of salt*

*1 tbs lemon juice * 1 cup sherry*

2 tbs gelatin

METHOD: Bring the white
wine to a boil and add the cranberries, mashing
slightly to mix with the wine. Simmer for 30
minutes. Strain through a double thickness of
cheesecloth, squeezing the berries to extract as
much juice as possible (the pulp can be kept
to make fruit cheese). Strain the juice a second
time into a pan and add the sugar, salt, lemon
juice, and sherry, and simmer for 5 minutes.
Remove from the heat. Dissolve the gelatin
in ¼ cup cold water and stir into the sherry-
cranberry mixture. Stir thoroughly. Allow the
jelly to cool, pour into prepared jars, and
seal. *Yield: 2–3 cups*

FRUIT
CHEESE

*f*ruit cheeses are a
delicious solution to the problem of putting away
large quantities of fruits at season's peak. The
pulp of many fruits—blackberries, plums,
apricots, apples—can be used to make a sweet,
dense, jelly-like 'cheese.' But because a large
amount is needed to make a small cheese, you
should use fruits when they are most plentiful.
Keep at least 2 months before serving; serve
sliced with hot or cold meats, as a dessert with
cream, or on bread or scones.

fruit (apples, plums, pears, etc),
a minimum of 3 lbs

sugar
(pound for pound with the fruit pulp)

METHOD: If you are using
fresh fruit, wash and clean (slice apples and pears),
then cover with water and bring to a boil in
a large pan. When tender, pass through a sieve
and discard the skins and stones. Put the weighed
pulp into a pan and, pound for pound, stir in
an equal amount of sugar. Heat gently and
stir frequently until the sugar is fully dissolved;
then cook for 45 minutes to 1 hour (stirring
frequently to prevent the sugar from burning).
When the cheese is cooked it will be quite stiff.
Pot and seal.

AUTUMN

HOLIDAY FRUITCAKE

This mildly spicy fruitcake can be served sliced thin and toasted as an accompaniment to spiced tea, or just plain. To present this gift, sprinkle the cake with dry sherry, brush with heated apricot or peach preserves, and decorate with pecans, almonds, and slivers of dried apricots. Surround with fresh mint or place on a doily-covered platter.

1 cup butter

*1 cup sugar * 2 eggs * ½ cup milk*

1¾ cups currants

1¼ cups mixed candied citrus peel

½ grated nutmeg pod

1 cup slivered almonds

*1 lemon, zest and juice * 1¾ cups flour*

dry sherry for sprinkling

METHOD: Generously grease and line with parchment paper an 8-inch round pan, or grease and flour a 5-cup ring mold; set

aside. Cream the butter and gradually add the
sugar, beating until the mixture is light and fluffy.
Add the eggs one at a time, beating well after
each addition. Add the milk. In a separate bowl,
combine the currants, candied peel, nutmeg,
almonds, and lemon zest with ¾ cup of flour. Add
the remaining cup of flour and lemon juice
to the egg batter; mix well. Fold in the fruit and
nut mixture. Pour into a prepared pan and
bake in a 300°F oven for 2 hours or until a fine
skewer inserted into the cake comes out clean.

Loosen the edges of the cake from the
pan or mold with a knife and allow to cool on a
wire rack before unmolding. Sprinkle the cake
with a little sherry, allow to cool completely.
Wrapped well and refrigerated, it will keep
for several weeks.

SIMCA'S HERBS

Assisting Simone Beck with her cooking classes in southern France over the years has been a great delight. I look forward to autumn in Provence, the smell of wild herbs, olive trees, and grapevines, not to mention the time spent with Simca and her husband Jean. Simca has called this marvelous combination of herbs, which she uses by the handful in lamb stews, sauces, and cheese tarts, MOTTS . . . Marjoram, Oregano, Twice Thyme, and Savory. Use only freshly dried herbs and no doubt "Simca's Herbs" will become a permanent fixture on your spice rack.

1 part marjoram

1 part oregano

2 parts thyme

1 part savory

METHOD: Combine all the herbs in a food processor or blender, then pass through a medium-fine sieve. Store in a tightly covered jar, in a cool place out of direct sunlight.

MARINATED
GOAT
CHEESE

*M*arinating in oil and herbs is a traditional way of preserving and flavoring goat cheese. Several small *chèvres* marinated in this way make a wonderful gift for any cheese-lover (cheeses can be replaced as they are eaten, or the oil strained and used in salad dressing). Follow the recipe below or try using a single herb, like several sprigs of rosemary or tarragon, or just 3 dried chili peppers. Store in the refrigerator, and allow at least 2 weeks to mature; they will last 6–8 weeks.

4 small round goat cheeses, 2–3 oz each

*1 bay leaf * 2 sprigs thyme*

*1 small sprig sage * 1 tsp black peppercorns*

2 cloves garlic, peeled

1 long strip lemon peel

good quality olive oil

METHOD: Place the cheeses, herbs, garlic, and lemon peel in a 1-quart jar with a tight fitting lid. Pour over enough olive oil (about 1½ cups) to cover the cheese generously. Cover tightly and store in the refrigerator.

JENNIFER'S LEMON CURD

my sister-in-law is a marvelous cook, and, being English, adds wonderful surprises to our family's table. Her lemon curd is one of my favorites. A curd is usually thicker and richer than jam, and in her recipe the richness is always balanced by the fresh tang of the lemons. I use it to fill tiny dessert pastry shells, topping each with a toasted pecan, and of course spread it on toast or scones.

4 medium lemons, zest and juice

¼ cup butter, cut into pieces

1¼ cups sugar

4 eggs, lightly beaten

METHOD: In a double boiler over simmering water combine the lemon zest, juice, butter, and sugar, stirring until all the butter has melted. Strain the beaten eggs into the lemon mixture. Stir continuously with a wooden spoon over a medium-to-low heat until the mixture is quite thick—it should be able to coat the back of the spoon. (Be careful not to overcook or the curd will separate.) Remove from heat, pour into prepared jars (the curd will thicken as it cools), seal, and store in a refrigerator. Keeps up to 3 months. *Yield: 2–3 cups*

POTTED SHRIMPS

Potted shrimps are a traditional English savory spread, served with brown bread and butter, or wholewheat toast with slices of lemon as part of an hors d'oeuvre, or as a light snack.

½ cup butter

1 lb peeled shrimps

¼ tsp powdered mace

¼ tsp cayenne pepper

salt and freshly ground black pepper

clarified butter

METHOD: Melt the butter over moderate heat. Stir in the shrimps, mace, and cayenne pepper. Continue stirring until the mixture is heated through, but do not allow to boil. Add salt and pepper to taste. Pour into small pots or crocks and seal with clarified butter. Will keep in the refrigerator for up to 2 weeks.
Yield: about 3 cups

WALNUT
GARLIC
OIL

Once you have had this oil around your kitchen, you will wonder how you ever did without it! Its subtle flavors enhance sautéed meats, salads, or marinades. Use a light French olive oil instead of the vegetable oil if you prefer.

5 cloves garlic, peeled and halved

8 walnut halves

2 cups vegetable oil

METHOD: Drop the garlic and walnut halves into a pint bottle. Warm the oil slightly and pour into the bottle. Seal and store in a cool place for at least a week, to allow the flavors to penetrate the oil.

AUTUMN

CHOCOLATE CHESTNUT TRUFFLES

These heavenly truffles are a little time-consuming but repay the effort. With fresh chestnuts, the truffles are richer-tasting than with canned. For variety, add finely chopped toasted almonds or freshly grated nutmeg to the truffle mixture.

6 oz bittersweet or semi-sweet chocolate

1 16-oz can whole chestnuts, or 1¼ lb fresh

*6 tbs butter * ½ cup sugar*

2½ tbs brandy or other liqueur

1 tsp vanilla

For the coating:

14 oz semi-sweet chocolate

1–1½ cups pure cocoa powder

METHOD: To prepare centers, melt chocolate in a double boiler and allow to cool. If using fresh chestnuts, cut a cross on the flat side of each shell, put in a large pan, cover with cold water, and boil for 5 minutes. Remove the shells and inner skins. Rice the chestnuts. Cream the butter and sugar together until fluffy, about 3 minutes. Add chestnuts and flavorings to the butter/sugar mixture and blend well, then stir in the cooled chocolate. Mix well. Roll into balls 1½ inches in diameter; if mixture becomes too soft to shape, chill for several minutes.

To coat, melt the chocolate on a plate over boiling water; let cool. Carefully roll the truffles in melted chocolate, then place on a plate of cocoa powder and allow to dry for several minutes. Dust each truffle with cocoa and place in paper candy cup. Store in refrigerator. *Yield: 5 dozen truffles*

AUTUMN

APPLE
MINT
JELLY

classic combination of tastes, this sweet jelly can be made slightly spicier by adding 1 tsp cinnamon, or ½ tsp ground allspice, or ½ tsp nutmeg to the apples while they are cooking.

3 lbs tart apples

*juice from 2 lemons * 1½ cups water*

½ cup fresh mint, washed and chopped

*2 cups cider vinegar * 1½–2½ cups sugar*

2 tbs fresh mint, finely chopped

METHOD: Wash, peel, core, and dice the apples. Place them in a large stainless steel pan, add the lemon juice, water, and ½ cup mint; bring to a boil. Cover and simmer until the apples are reduced to a pulp (about 15-20 minutes). Strain the mixture overnight through a jelly bag or sieve lined with a double layer of cheesecloth over a bowl. For every 2 cups of juice obtained, add 1½ cups sugar. Stir the mixture over a low heat until the sugar has dissolved, then boil until the liquid begins to set (it should coat the back of a spoon). Skim the jelly periodically during cooking. Remove from the heat, add the remaining chopped mint, and stir. Allow to cool before pouring into prepared jars. *Yield: 2–3 cups*

AUTUMN

HERB-
FLAVORED
BUTTERS

Flavored butters
enhance so many dishes; try them on filet mignon,
fresh steamed asparagus, or with smoked salmon
as an hors d'oeuvre. To use as a garnish, roll into
a log and slice.

½ lb butter

3 tbs parsley, finely chopped

¼ tsp freshly ground white pepper

2 tbs fresh tarragon, or
thyme, or sage, or
1 good sized garlic clove, minced and mashed, or
2 tbs chives, finely minced, or
1 tbs horseradish, freshly grated or
2 anchovy fillets

METHOD: Mix the butter,
parsley, pepper, and chosen flavor together in a
bowl with a fork. Pack the butter into several
small crocks and cover or roll into a log and
wrap tightly. Store in the refrigerator or freeze.
Yield: 1 cup

Winter

ABBY'S BUTTER TOFFEE

gift of this toffee has become a delicious Christmas tradition in our family. My sister gathers charming old tins throughout the year and fills them with her wonderful toffee to send to friends for the holidays.

2 cups sugar ✻ *½ cup water*

1¼ cups light corn syrup ✻ *1 cup butter*

1¾ cups chopped almonds

For the topping:

10 oz bittersweet or semi-sweet chocolate, coarsely chopped

1 cup chopped almonds

METHOD: Butter two 8-inch square pans. Combine the sugar, water, corn syrup, and butter in a heavy-based saucepan. Over medium heat, bring to the hard crack stage (295°F), stirring occasionally. Remove from heat immediately. Stir in 1¼ cups almonds and pour into the prepared pans. Sprinkle chocolate over the hot toffee, spread evenly, and top with remaining chopped almonds. Allow to cool and break into small pieces. Store in an airtight container. *Yield: 3–3½ lbs.*

COCONUT MERINGUE KISSES

eringues should be as delicate in texture as in flavor. In this recipe, the whites of large eggs are used and the sugar is superfine to dissolve quickly.

*¾ cup water * 1 cup superfine sugar*

*4 egg whites * ⅛ tsp cream of tartar * 1 tsp vanilla*

¾ cup flaked coconut, unsweetened

METHOD: Butter a baking sheet and cover it with parchment paper; butter and flour the paper. In a heavy saucepan, heat water and sugar until the sugar dissolves, and boil to soft-ball stage (238°F). Meanwhile, beat the egg whites with an electric mixer until frothy. Add cream of tartar and continue beating until the mixture forms soft peaks. With mixer running, dribble the hot syrup into the egg whites and continue beating rapidly until the meringue cools and forms stiff peaks, about 8–10 minutes. Stir in vanilla and coconut. Spoon meringue into a pastry bag fitted with a ½-inch star tip. Pipe small round kisses approximately 1½ inches in diameter onto the sheet, leaving about a 1-inch space between.

Bake in a 200°F oven for 1½–2 hours, or until the meringues are light and dry (the low oven prevents browning). Loosen immediately and allow to cool on the sheet. *Yield: 6 dozen*

CANDIED CITRUS PEEL

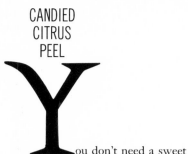

ou don't need a sweet tooth to enjoy candied citrus peel. As a garnish, topping a fruit sorbet, added to a glass of sparkling wine, or served alone at the end of a meal, they are eye-catching and unusual delicacies. Try the more exotic citrus fruits when you can find them: citron; clementines, a hybrid of bitter Seville oranges and tangerines; and uglis, the green and orange offspring of grapefruit and tangelo.

2 large grapefruits

2 lemons

2 limes

4 oranges or tangellos

⅓ cup light corn syrup

2 cups sugar

1 cup hot water

granulated sugar for rolling

METHOD: Wash the fruit and with a sharp knife remove the peel in segments, about a quarter of the whole fruit at a time. Remove as much of the pulp and white membrane as possible and cut peel into ¼-inch wide

strips. Put into a pan, cover with cold water
and bring to a boil. Cook for 15–20 minutes, drain
off the water. Repeat and boil until the peel
is tender (about another 15 minutes). Drain, cool,
and remove any white membrane left on the slices.

Combine the corn syrup, sugar, and hot
water in a saucepan and cook until the sugar has
dissolved. Add the sliced peel and cook until
the syrup forms a very soft ball (236°F) when
dropped into cold water, about 40 minutes. The
peel will appear transparent. Remove the pieces
from the syrup and place on a rack to drain.
Roll each strip in granulated sugar. Store in layers
separated by wax paper in a tin with a tight
fitting lid. *Yield: 2½ cups*

WINTER

73

FLAVORED MUSTARDS

lavoring mustards is quite simple, and there is no end to the varieties you can create. Citrus mustards make good additions to sauces for shellfish; herbed mustards are perfect with sausages or as a base for salad dressings; hot, spiced mustards give a zing to ham or prime rib. All the quantities below are for an 8-oz jar of Dijon mustard.

Citrus mustard:

2 tsp freshly grated lemon or orange zest

½ tsp lemon or orange extract

Herb mustard:

*½ tsp oregano * 1 tsp thyme * ½ tsp tarragon*

Spice mustard:

¼ tsp dried chili pepper flakes

*1 tsp finely minced shallot * fresh nutmeg, about 2 'grates'*

METHOD: Put the mustard
into a 2-cup bowl. Stir in the desired flavors, mix well and return to the original jar or a decorative jar with a tight stopper. Keep refrigerated at least 3 weeks before serving.

CUMBERLAND SAUCE

This sweet, port-flavored sauce is originally English. As a glaze, it can be brushed over the skin of a roasting chicken, or drizzled over sliced venison or duck, but it also makes a colorful and tasty garnish for any meat. When red currant jelly can't be found, substitute a good raspberry or blackberry jelly.

1 cup red currant jelly

½ tsp English mustard

¼ cup port

¼ cup orange juice, freshly squeezed

2 tbs lemon juice

2 medium-sized shallots

zest of ½ orange

METHOD: Heat the jelly slightly. Whisk in the mustard, port, and orange and lemon juice. Peel and finely mince the shallots and blanch by dropping them into rapidly boiling water for 30 seconds. Drain through a fine sieve and whisk with the orange zest into the sauce; pour into prepared jars. *Yield: 3 cups*

WINTER
WINE
SPICES

ulled wine is a particularly warming drink for winter evenings, and a delicious way of improving a poor wine, too. Add 2 teaspoons of the spice mixture and 3–4 slices of orange for each bottle of red wine, warm over a low heat for 20–30 minutes, strain, and serve. (A cup of sherry can be added just before serving the wine—this will increase its potency considerably!)

5 cinnamon sticks

1 whole nutmeg

⅓ cup whole cloves

⅛ cup whole allspice

¼ cup dried orange peel

METHOD: Break up the
cinnamon sticks by placing a plate over them and pressing down. Crack the nutmeg and cut into small pieces and crush the cloves and allspice. Mix all the spices together with the orange peel and store in an airtight container. *Yield: ¾ cup*

OREGON PRUNE JAM

Prunes' sweet, almost earthy flavor make delectable jam. This is delicious on corn muffins, combined with apples for a pie, or folded into whipped cream. Toss in a few toasted, halved hazelnuts and use several tablespoons in roast goose stuffing. Reduce the amount of sugar if you prefer.

2½ lbs pitted prunes

*2½–3 cups sugar * ½ tsp allspice*

*½ tsp cloves * ½ tsp cinnamon * ¼ tsp nutmeg*

1 cup cider vinegar

METHOD: In a bowl, mix the pitted prunes, sugar, and spices together. Pour the vinegar into a stainless steel saucepan, add the prune mixture, and cook slowly over low heat, stirring frequently to prevent sticking, until the jam thickens and coats the back of a spoon. Pour into prepared jars and cover tightly. *Yield: 4 cups*

WINTER

CHOCOLATE
WHISKY
BALLS

 variation of the classic Bourbon Balls, the chocolate cookie crumbs make these sinfully rich and *very* chocolatey! Substitute your favorite liquor for the whisky, or roll them in finely chopped pecans instead of sugar, if you prefer. These keep well and are marvellous with eggnog.

1 cup pecans

1 cup chocolate wafer cookie crumbs

1 cup confectioners sugar

1½ tbs light corn syrup

¼ cup whisky

powdered sugar for rolling

METHOD: Grind the pecans and the chocolate wafers coarsely in a food processor and empty into a large bowl. Mix in the sugar, corn syrup, and whisky very thoroughly (I use my hands). Shape the mixture into balls the size of a quarter and roll in powdered sugar. Keep in an airtight container in a cool place, or freeze on a baking sheet until each is firm and store in tightly sealed plastic bags. *Yield: 2–3 dozen*

CHRISTMAS PUDDING

This recipe makes three puddings; certainly you will want to keep at least one for yourself. There is no reason to make this only for Christmas; serve it with brandy or rum butter (see page 82) any time of the year. Wrapped in cheesecloth and foil, the puddings will keep 4–6 months.

1 lb seedless raisins

1 lb currants ✳ *½ lb walnuts or pecans, chopped*

⅓ lb candied citrus peel

6 eggs ✳ *2 cups dark molasses*

½ cup peanut oil ✳ *2 cups fresh breadcrumbs*

½ cup flour ✳ *1½ cups wholewheat flour*

1 tsp baking soda ✳ *1 tsp salt*

*½ tsp each nutmeg, cinnamon,
cloves, and allspice*

2 cups buttermilk ✳ *½ cup brandy*

METHOD: Dust the fruit and nuts with a little of the flour. In a large bowl, beat the eggs and add the molasses, oil, breadcrumbs, and floured fruit.

In a separate bowl, mix the dry ingredients
together and add alternately to the fruit/egg
mixture with the buttermilk and brandy, stirring
well with a wooden spoon. Grease three 5-cup
molds and fill two-thirds full with the mixture.
Cover with tight fitting lids, or a double layer of
foil. Place the puddings in a roasting pan and
surround with hot water (the water should come
about one-third up the sides of the molds).
Cover the entire pan with foil and poke two holes
for steam. Steam in a 300°F oven for 3 hours,
checking regularly that the water has not simmered
away and refilling with boiling water as necessary.

Remove the puddings, cool, and wrap in
brandy-soaked cheesecloth, then in aluminum
foil, and store. To serve, remove the cheesecloth,
rewrap the puddings in foil, and reheat in a
steamer over simmering water for 1 hour. Decorate
with candied citrus peel, brandied cherries, or
toasted slivered almonds.

BRANDY
BUTTER

classic
accompaniment to fruitcakes, mincepies, and
Christmas pudding, this sweet butter can also be
made with rum or even Grand Marnier. It freezes
well and will keep for several months if sealed
tightly. Serve at room temperature, when it
should be spreadable.

¾ cup butter

1 cup powdered sugar

grated zest of 1 large lemon

3 tbs brandy

METHOD: Beat the butter
until soft and light. Gradually add the sugar and
continue beating. Add the lemon zest and brandy,
and mix well. Pack into a crock, cover, and
freeze. *Yield: 1¾ cups*

WALNUT CRANBERRY BREAD

This is my husband's favorite quick bread; the piquant combination of flavors is lovely as morning toast, an afternoon accompaniment to tea, and as a holiday bread at Christmas. Frozen cranberries work very nicely and, if the bread is well-wrapped, it can be frozen for several months.

*2 tbs butter * 1 cup sugar*

1 egg, lightly beaten

*2 oranges, zested * ³/₄ cup orange juice*

*2 cups flour * ¹/₂ tsp salt * ¹/₂ tsp baking soda*

1¹/₂ tsp baking powder

1 cup whole cranberries

³/₄ cup chopped walnuts

METHOD: Cream the
butter and sugar together, add the beaten egg, then the orange juice and zest. Sift the remaining dry ingredients together. Dust the cranberries and nuts with 1 extra tablespoon flour. Blend the sugar-orange mixture with the sifted dry ingredients. Stir in the nuts and cranberries. Pour batter into a medium loaf pan that has been greased and floured; bake at 325°F for 1–1¹/₄ hours.

VALENTINE SHORTBREAD

lmost everyone adores shortbread. For this festive St. Valentine's version, use heart-shaped cookie cutters, and trim with red and silver decorations.

*1½ cups butter * 1 cup sugar * 4 cups flour, sifted*

For the decoration:

*½ cup apricot jam * red and silver candies*

METHOD: Beat the butter with an electric mixer for 5 minutes, until it is light and fluffy. Gradually add the sugar, then the flour, mixing well. Knead the dough until smooth; shape into a ball and cut in half. Press half the dough into a rectangle about ½-inch thick on an ungreased baking sheet. Cut into desired shapes. Prick the surface well and bake in a 300°F oven for 30–45 minutes, or until the edges are light brown. Remove from the baking sheet and place on a rack to cool, handling carefully as the shortbread is quite fragile.

To serve, heat the apricot jam in a small pan until just boiling. Strain and brush over the shortbread. Decorate the edges with red and silver candies (when hardened the jam will hold the candies in place). Stored tightly wrapped in foil or in an airtight container without the decoration, the shortbread will keep for up to 10 days.
Yield: 4–5 dozen cookies

PRESENTATION & PRESERVATION

Presentation

*

Presentation makes all the difference to food, and this applies as much to a jam, chutney, or cake given as a gift as it does to a meal served at the table. A jar of favorite preserves or a batch of cookies is a thoughtful gift to a neighbor or weekend hostess, but wrapped with a little imagination it can be turned into something really special! With so many different colors and patterns of paper, cellophanes, fabrics, boxes, and ribbons available, the possibilities are endless.

Store-bought wrapping paper, and even plain brown paper, can be attractively personalized in many ways. With rubber stamps, stencils, spray paint, felt markers, or a box of crayons you can create your own distinctive 'one-off' patterns and designs for paper and cards. This really does not require a lot of time or great artistic ability: it is surprising how effective a few splashes of bright color on plain paper can be. (Children always rise to the challenge of creating unique decorations, so put their imagination and energy to work.)

PRESENTATION

Put aside bottles and jars and crocks throughout the year. For very special gifts, you can sometimes find old glass jars or even decanters in antique or junk shops that can be filled with a favorite preserve or liquor. Tins and boxes, particularly those with attractive patterns, are worth saving, and I always keep an eye out for unusual designs and shapes. A little paint or self-adhesive paper will improve their appearance, if necessary.

A variety of cardboard boxes can be found in stationery and card shops and department stores (often the boxes cosmetics are sold in can be adapted, but avoid those with lingering fragrance). Wicker baskets and hampers make good containers for cakes, breads, and cookies; or selections of jams, preserves, or various gifts. Baked goods will stay fresh longer if they're wrapped in cellophane and sealed, perhaps with a ribbon. Individual candies look pretty and are easier to handle if they're in little paper candy cups in a tin or box, the layers separated by wax paper.

PRESENTATION

Don't forget to label your gifts clearly; this can be a further decorative element. Instead of using a stick-on label, you may prefer to put the information on a small gift card or tag and tie it to the container with a narrow ribbon or silk cord.

Once inside a box, tin, hamper, or any other container, surround your gift with colored tissue paper or cellophane or flowers or, especially in autumn, some leaves. Pack anything you plan to send through the mail very well. During World War II, many people sent cakes and cookies overseas packed in plain popcorn. Today we have the convenience of styrofoam. Use a strong cardboard box and line well with the styrofoam (or plastic bubbles, or balls of newspaper), place the gift in the center and surround with more packing, filling the box tightly before sealing. Finally, label clearly with a return address.

Preservation

*

Most of the foods in this book are designed to be kept for at least a few days, some for several months, if stored properly. But unless it is stored correctly, any food will deteriorate fairly quickly, and there are few greater disappointments than finding a batch of cookies or several jars of jam have spoiled because of poor storage.

Breads, cakes, and cookies are the most perishable of the foods in this book and should be stored in tightly-sealed containers in a cool, dry place, or wrapped in foil and frozen if you want to keep longer. Any decorations— icings, glazes—or fillings should be added just before use. Candies should also be stored in tightly-sealed containers, separated in layers by wax paper, and kept in a cool, dry place. Humidity will reduce the keeping time of all unfrozen baked goods.

Salmon butter and any potted meat or fish are also highly perishable and should be refrigerated in crocks or pots and sealed with clarified butter. Although it is simple to make, I always keep a batch of clarified butter in the refrigerator and heat before use. To clarify, melt butter in a small pan. Skim off any foam that has accumulated on top, pour off and reserve the clear liquid, and discard the milky solids in the bottom of the pan. Pour the clarified butter over potted food and when cool, it will form a thin, edible seal.

Sterilization

All preserves—jams, jellies, pickles, and chutneys—should be stored in sterilized glass containers. Ideally, you should use proper Mason or Ball-type preserving jars. They are made of thicker glass, to withstand the heat of sterilization, and have either clip-on or screw-on airtight lids with rubber sealing rings to ensure a tight seal. I never seem to have enough of these containers in the house. But they can be used over and over again (only the rubber sealing rings need replacing occasionally), and I find it economical to buy them by the case.

Empty jars and bottles, particularly when they have interesting shapes, can be used for preserves if they are free of cracks or chips and can withstand sterilization. Use these jars if only a scalding is needed to sterilize, such as when a vinegar-based relish or chutney, or a liquor-based sauce is being stored in a refrigerator. Make sure that the lid is airtight and remove any cardboard liners (a piece of plastic wrap will improve the seal).

To sterilize your containers, wash first in warm, soapy water and rinse well. Stand upright on a low rack or folded towel in the bottom of a large pot or canning kettle. Pour 1–2 inches of hot water into the pot and cover with a tight-fitting lid. About 30 minutes before the preserve is ready, bring the water to a boil over medium heat. Lower the heat and simmer 15 minutes, checking to make sure that the water does not boil away and adding more, if necessary. In a separate saucepan, boil the washed and rinsed lids for 5 minutes; leave in the water until needed.

When the preserve is ready, remove the jars from the pan using a pair of tongs. Empty of any water, place on a wooden or non-metallic surface, and fill to about ⅛ inch of the top. The jars should still be hot when filled with food so that the glass does not shatter. Wipe the rim free of any drips, immediately cover with the hot lids, and screw on tightly. Let the jars cool completely before storing as directed. (Jams or preserves containing whole fruits or herbs or other solids, like rose petal jam, should be allowed to cool for about 10 minutes before sealing so that the solids are evenly suspended and do not rise to the top).

Label each jar clearly, with the name of the recipe, the date it was made and the date it should be eaten by, and any special storing or serving suggestions.

Equipment

Few of the recipes in this book require special equipment beyond that normally found in any working kitchen.

For jams and jellies, a jelly bag or a colander or fine-mesh strainer lined with several layers of cheesecloth is necessary to strain the fruit.

When working with fruits, vinegar-based relishes, and other acidic ingredients, use stainless-steel or stainless-steel lined cookware—never iron pans or carbon steel knives, which will discolor and flavor the preserve.

A double boiler should be used when melting chocolate or for cooking mixtures with eggs, as both ingredients are easily scorched by direct heat. If you don't have a double boiler, you can create your own by placing one pan inside another containing enough water to touch the bottom and rise about ½ inch up the side of the small pan.

For some candies, a candy thermometer is particularly useful, as exact temperatures are very important. If you haven't a thermometer, though, you can judge the temperature of the mixture from its reaction in cold water. Simple drop ½ teaspoon of the hot candy mixture into a small amount of cold water and look for the desired consistency:

stage	cold-water test	temperature
thread	syrup runs off in a 2-inch thread as it is dropped from metal spoon	230–234°F.
soft ball	syrup can be shaped into ball in water, flattens when removed from water	234–240°F.
firm ball	syrup can be shaped into firm ball in water, does not flatten when removed	244–248°F.
hard ball	syrup forms hard, but still pliable, ball	250–266°F.
soft crack	syrup separates into firm, but not brittle, threads in water	270–290°F.
hard crack	syrup separates into hard, brittle threads	300–310°F.

Index of Recipes

*